Academy Stars

Pupil's Book

S Starter

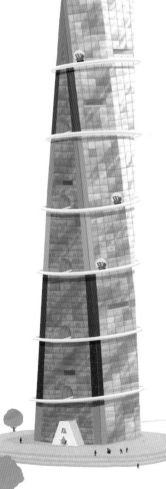

macmillan
education

Scope and sequence

Grammar	Speaking and Listening
Ask and answer about personal details: *What's your name? My name's … How old are you? I'm …* Give personal details: *I'm eight.*	Ask and answer about age: *How old are you? I'm five.* Listen for key words
Talk about feelings: *I'm scared.* Ask and answer about feelings: *How are you? I'm happy.*	Ask and answer about feelings: *Are you angry? Yes, I am. / No, I'm not.* Listen for key words
Talk about classroom objects: *This is my pen.* Describe classroom objects: *I've got a rubber.*	Talk about your classroom objects: *This is my notebook. I've got a backpack.* Listen for key words
Talk about favourite colours: *What colour is it? It's pink. My favourite colour is pink.* Talk about colours: *I've got a pen. What colour is it? It's blue.*	Ask and answer about colours: *What's your favourite colour? My favourite colour is yellow.* Listen for key words
Describe clothes: *My shirt is blue.* Describe clothes: *My socks are red.*	Ask and answer about clothes: *I've got a new skirt. What colour is it? It's purple.* Listen for key words
Describe parts of the body: *I've got two hands.* Talk about parts of the body: *This is my nose. These are my ears.*	Talk about yourself: *This is my hand. I've got two hands.* Listen for key words
Describe how family members feel: *My brother is scared.* Introduce family members and say how they feel: *These are my uncle and aunt. They're happy.*	Introduce your family members to a friend: *This is my brother. Hello! Nice to meet you.* Listen for key words
Ask and answer about animals: *What is it? It's a duck. What are they? They're sheep.* Ask and answer about animals: *Is it a duck? Yes, it is. / No, it isn't.*	Ask and answer to guess an animal: *Is it a cow? No, it isn't. Is it a rabbit? Yes, it is!* Listen for key words

Welcome

1 🔊 1.1 **Listen and point.**

Welcome Identify and use new words: classroom language

Lesson 1   Vocabulary

2 🔊 1.1 **Listen again and say.**

1 Hello!

Unit 1 Identify and use new words: numbers 1–10

1 🔊 1.2 **Listen and point.**

1 2 3 4 5
6 7 8 9 10

2 🔊 1.2 **Listen again and say.**

3 💡 **Look at the picture. Find, count and say the number.**

4 🔊 1.3 **Sing and act out.**

1   🔊 1.4   **Listen and follow.**

2   🔊 1.4   **Listen again. How old are they? Say.**

1    2    3    4

3   💬   **Work in groups. Act out the story.**    Be a star! ⭐

Lesson 4   Grammar

1 🔊 1.5 **Listen and match.**

2 **Look and say.**

1

2

3 👤 **Draw and say.** Be a star! ⭐

Lessons 1 and 2   Vocabulary

1  1.16 **Listen and point.**

2  1.16 **Listen again and say.**

3  **Look at the picture. Find, count and match.**

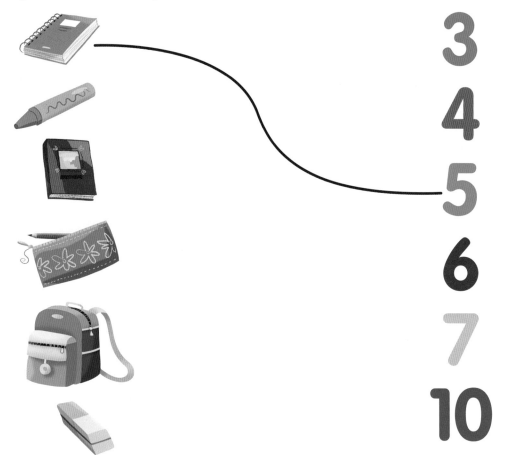

4 1.17 **Sing and act out.**  Be a star!

1 🔊 1.18 **Listen and follow.**

2 🔊 1.18 **Listen again. Circle blue for Jack and circle red for Maya.**

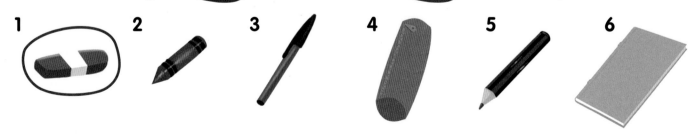

3 💬 **Work in groups. Act out the story.** Be a star! ⭐

Lesson 4   Grammar

1 🔊 1.19 **Listen and match.**

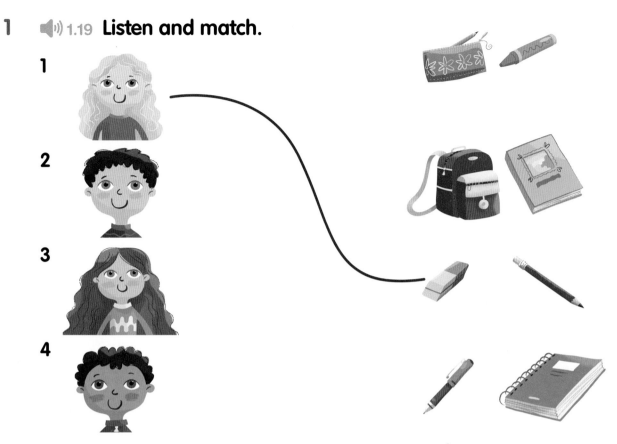

2 **Complete and colour. Then say.** | Be a star! ⭐ |

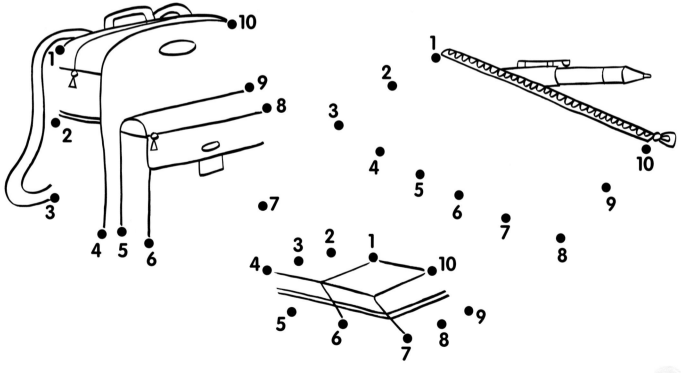

1 🔊 1.20 **Listen and say.**

2 💬 **Work in pairs. Talk about the classroom objects.**

3 💬 **Now it's your turn. Tell a friend about your classroom objects.** [Be a star! ⭐]

Lesson 6   Listening

1  1.21 **Listen and circle.**

1

2

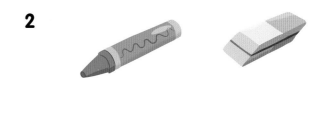

3

4

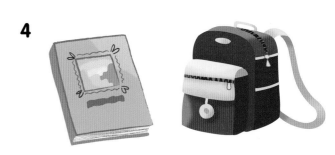

2 1.22 **Listen and tick (✓) the correct classroom objects.**

1

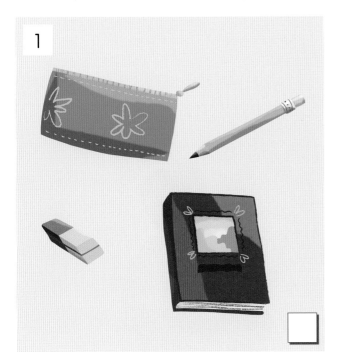

2

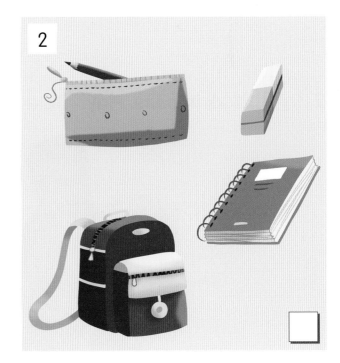

3 **Find classroom objects. Act out.** Be a star! ☆

1   Make a game.

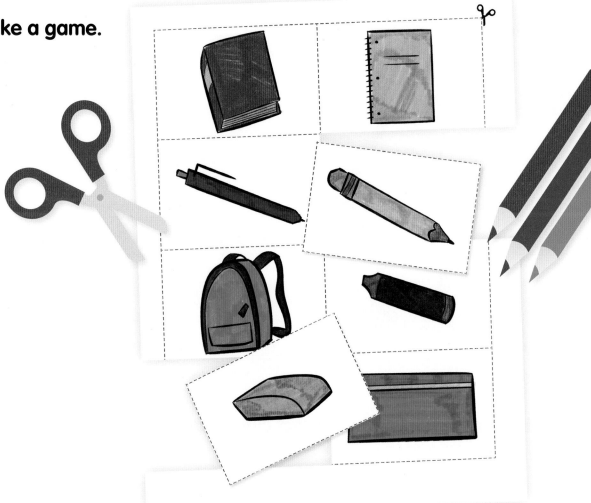

2   💬 Work in pairs. Play.   Be a star! ⭐

1 Find and (circle). Then say.

2 💬 Play *Memory*. Say the classroom objects. [Be a star! ⭐]

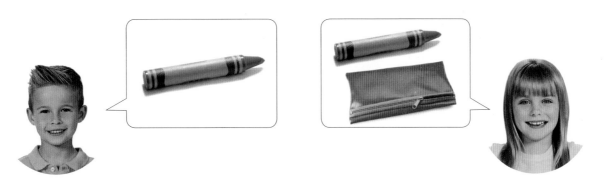

4 My favourite colours

Unit 4 Identify and use new words: colours

1    1.23 **Listen and point.**

2   (1)) 1.23 **Listen again and say.**

3   💡 **Look at the picture. Find and say.**

4   (1)) 1.24 **Sing and act out.**  Be a star! ⭐

1 🔊 **1.25 Listen and follow.**

2 Find and say. Then colour.

1

2

3

4

3 💬 **Work in groups. Act out the story.** Be a star! ⭐

1 🔊 1.26 **Listen and match. Then colour.**

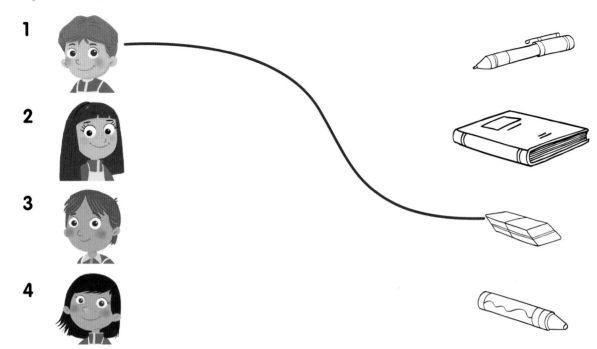

2 💡 **Choose and colour.**

1 = ⭐ 2 = ⭐ 3 = ⭐ 4 = ⭐

5 = ⭐ 6 = ⭐ 7 = ⭐ 8 = ⭐

3 👤 **Talk about your picture.** [Be a star! ⭐]

1   ◀)) 1.27 **Listen and say.**

2   **Work in pairs. Ask and answer.**

3   **Now it's your turn. Talk about your favourite colours.** Be a star! ☆

1 🔊 1.28 **Listen and ⟨circle⟩.**

1
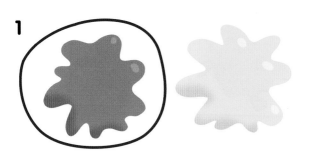

2
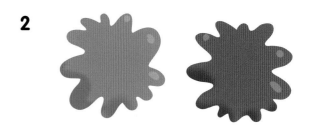

3

4
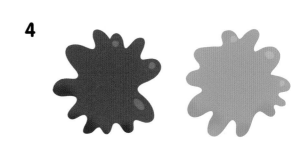

2 🔊 1.29 **Listen and tick (✓) the correct parrot.**

1

2

3 🗨 **Look at Activity 2. Choose a parrot. Act out.**  Be a star! ⭐

1   **Make a game.**

2   💬 **Work in pairs. Play.** Be a star! ⭐

1 **Find and point. Then say.**

2 **Colour. Then act out.** [Be a star! ⭐]

5 My clothes

Unit 5 Identify and use new words: clothes

1 1.30 **Listen and point.**

2 1.30 **Listen again and say.**

3 **Look at the picture. Find and say.**

4 1.31 **Sing and act out.** Be a star!

1　🔊 1.32 **Listen and follow.**

2　**Find and say. Then colour.**

1 　**2** 　**3** 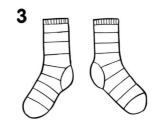　**4**

3　🗨 **Work in groups. Act out the story.** Be a star! ⭐

1   🔊 1.33 **Listen and match. Then colour.**

2   **Colour. Look and say.**

3   💡 **Draw and say.** [Be a star! ⭐]

1 🔊 1.34 **Listen and say.**

2 💬 **Work in pairs. Ask and answer.**

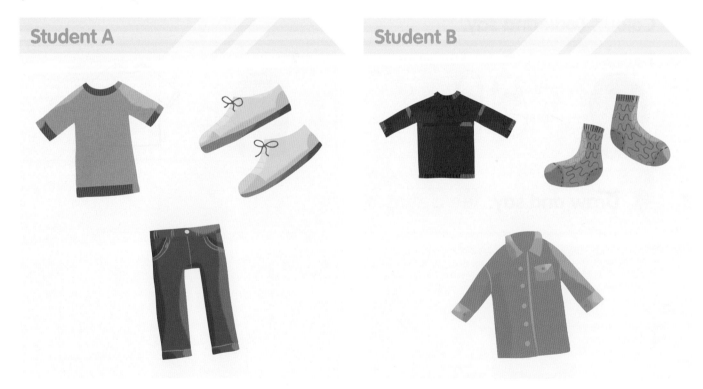

Student A

Student B

3 💬 **Now it's your turn. Talk about your new clothes.**

1 🔊 1.35 **Listen and circle.**

1   2

3   4

2 🔊 1.36 **Listen and tick (✓) the correct boy.**

1   2

3 💬 **Look at Activity 2. Choose a boy. Act out.** Be a star! ⭐

1   **Make a game.**

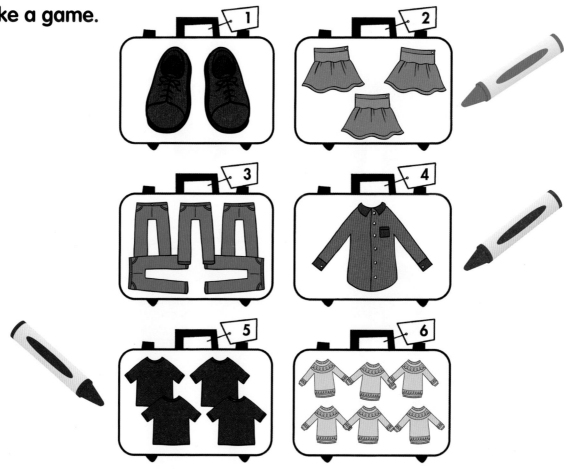

2   💬 **Work in pairs. Play.** Be a star! ⭐

1 **Find and (circle). Then say.**

2 💬 **Colour. Then act out.** [Be a star! ⭐]

6 This is me!

Unit 6 Identify and use new words: parts of the face

1   🔊 1.37 **Listen and point.**

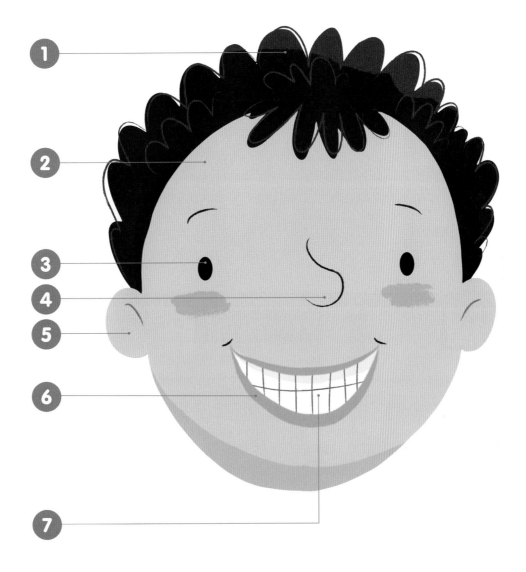

2   🔊 1.37 **Listen again and say.**

3   💡 **Look at the picture on page 46. Find and say the parts of the face.**

4   🔊 1.38 **Sing and act out.**   Be a star! ⭐

1   🔊 1.39 **Listen and follow.**

2   **Find.** Circle **blue for Jack and** circle **red for Maya. Then say.**

3   💬 **Work in groups. Act out the story.**  Be a star! ⭐

Unit 6 Describe parts of the body: *I've got two hands.*

1 🔊 1.40 **Listen and match.**

2 👤 **Draw a picture of you. Talk about it.** Be a star! ⭐

1 🔊 1.41 **Listen and say.**

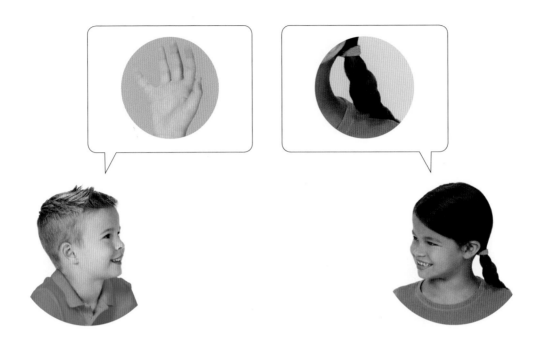

2 🗨 **Work in pairs. Talk about parts of the body.**

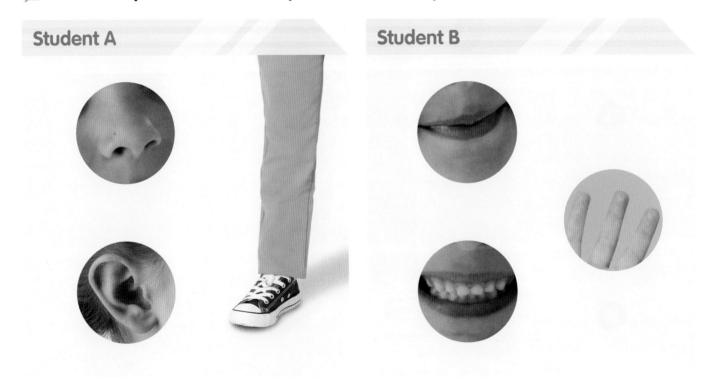

Student A

Student B

3 🗨 **Now it's your turn. Talk about you.** [Be a star! ⭐]

Lesson 6　　Listening

1 1.42 **Listen and circle.**

1
 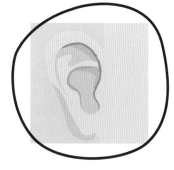

2

3

4

2 1.43 **Listen and tick (✓) the correct monster.**

1

2

3 **Look at Activity 2. Choose a monster. Act out.** Be a star! ⭐

1   **Make a game.**

2   💬 **Work in pairs. Play.** Be a star! ⭐

1   **Find and** (circle). **Then say.**

2   **Choose and act out.** [Be a star!] ☆

7 My family

Unit 7 Identify and use new words: family members

1   🔊 1.44 **Listen and point.**

2   🔊 1.44 **Listen again and say.**

3   💡 **Look at the picture. Find and say.**

4   🔊 1.45 **Sing and act out.** ⎡Be a star! ⭐⎤

1 🔊 1.46 **Listen and follow.**

2 💡 **Look at the pictures. How are they feeling? Find the family members and say.**

1  **2**  **3**  **4**

3 💬 **Work in groups. Act out the story.**

1 ◀)) 1.47 **Listen and match.**

2 **Look and say.**

3 👤 **Draw and say.** ⬚ Be a star! ⭐

1   🔊 1.48 **Listen and say.**

2   🗨 **Work in pairs. Talk about the family members.**

3   🗨 **Now it's your turn. Introduce your family.** [Be a star! ⭐]

Lesson 6   Listening

1 🔊 1.49 **Listen and (circle).**

1

2

3

4

2 🔊 1.50 **Listen and tick (✓) the correct family.**

1

2

3 💬 **Look at Activity 2. Choose a family. Act out.** [Be a star! ⭐]

1 Make a game.

2 Work in pairs. Play. Be a star! ☆

Unit 7 Play a game using the new language
Game template page 83

Lesson 8   Review

1 Find and (circle). Then say.

2 👤 💬 **Draw. Then act out.** Be a star! ⭐

1 🔊 1.51 **Listen and point.**

2 🔊 1.51 **Listen again and say.**

3 💡 **Look at the picture. Find and say.**

4 🔊 1.52 **Sing and act out.** **Be a star!** ⭐

1 🔊 1.53 **Listen and follow.**

2 **Number the animals in order.**

3 💬 **Work in groups. Act out the story.** (Be a star! ⭐)

Unit 8 Ask and answer about animals: *What is it? It's a duck. What are they? They're sheep.*

1 🔊 1.54 **Listen and circle.**

1

2

3

4

2 **Ask and answer.**

1

2

3 👤 **Draw and say.** [Be a star! ⭐]

1 🔊 1.55 **Listen and say.**

2 💬 **Work in pairs. Play** *Guess the animal.*

Student A

Student B

3 💬 **Now it's your turn. Play** *Guess the animal.* [Be a star! ⭐]

Lesson 6　　Listening

1　🔊 1.56 **Listen and ⟨circle⟩.**

1

2

3

4

2　🔊 1.57 **Listen and tick (✓) the correct farm.**

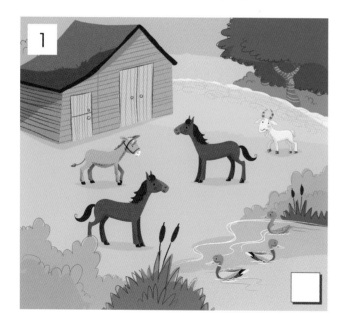

3　💬 **Look at Activity 2. Choose a farm. Act out.** ⟨Be a star! ⭐⟩

1   Make a game.

2   💬 Work in pairs. Play. [Be a star!] ⭐

1   **Find and** (circle). **Then count and say.**

2   **Say the number. Then guess.** [Be a star!] ⭐

Goodbye

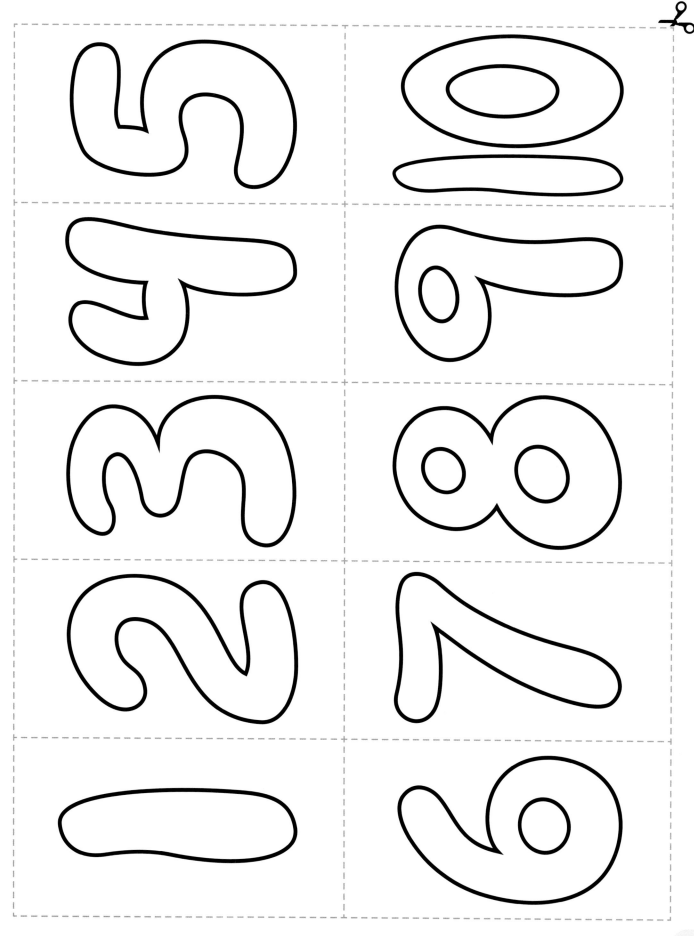

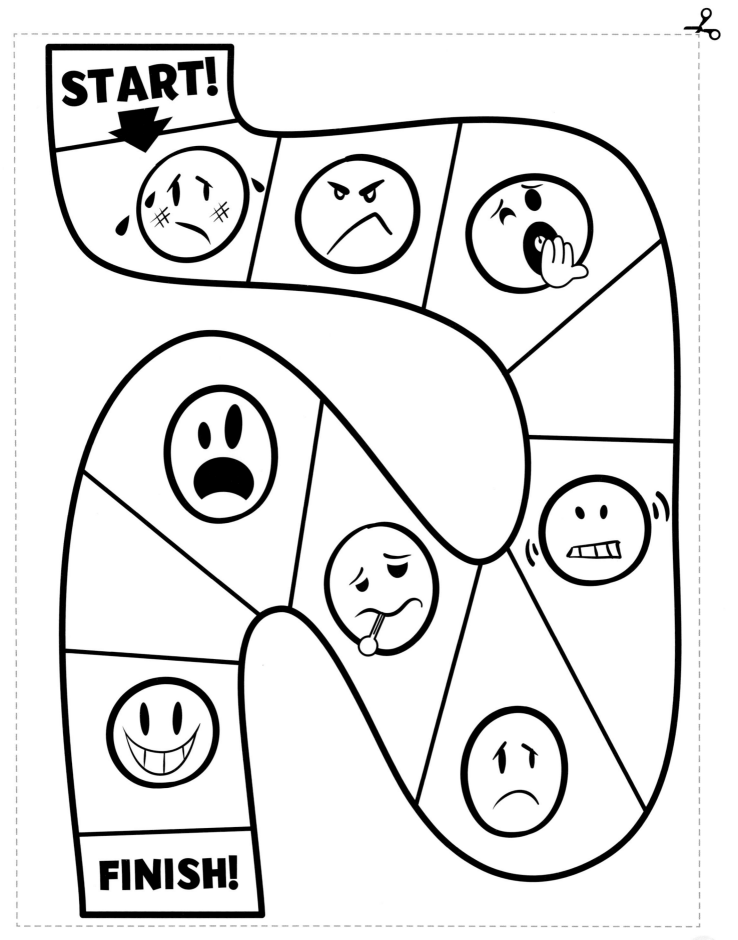

START!

FINISH!

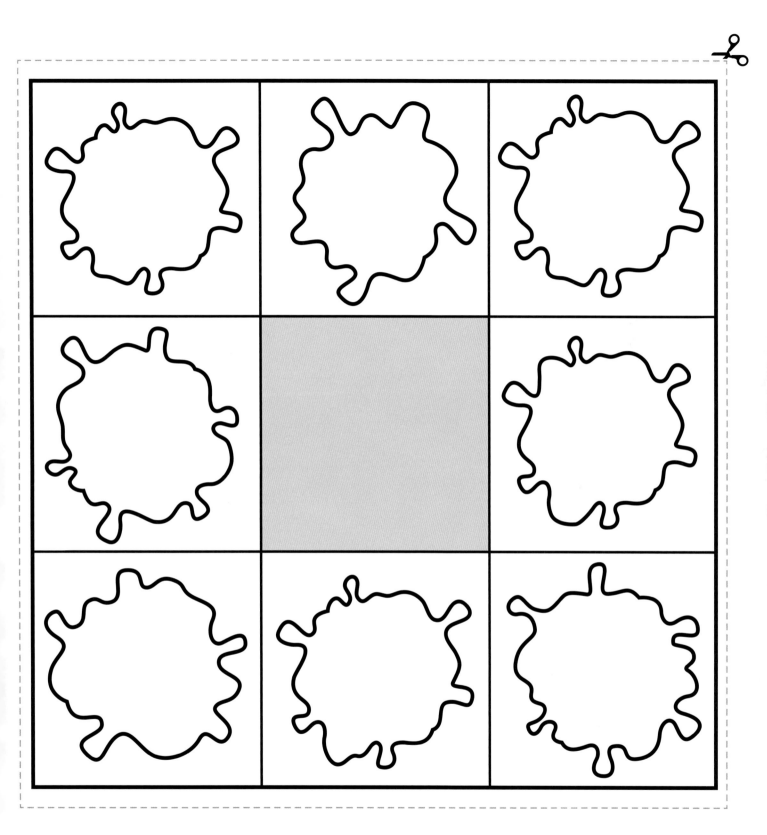

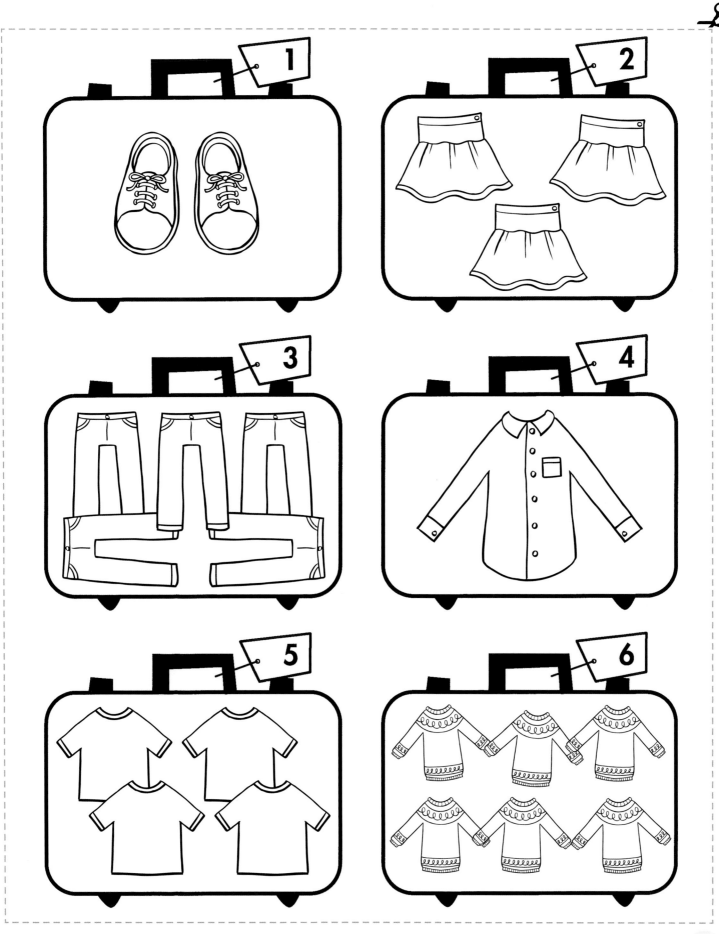

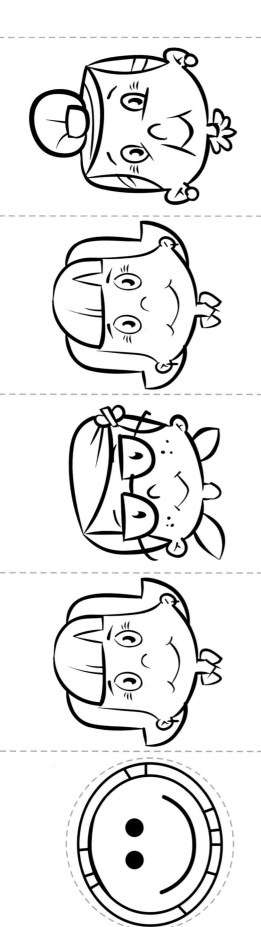
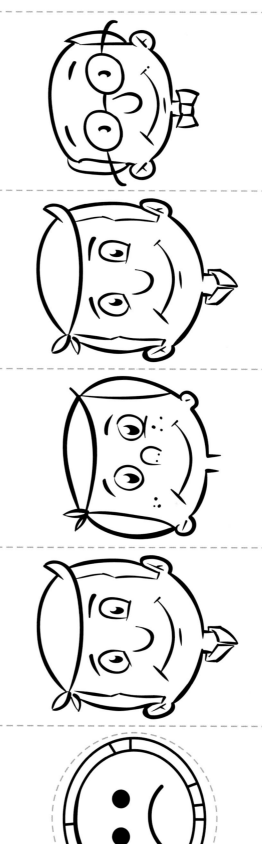

Picture dictionary

Welcome

1 2 3
4 5
6 7 8
9 10

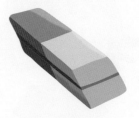

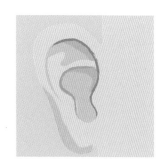

Macmillan Education
4 Crinan Street
London N1 9XW
A division of Springer Nature Limited

Companies and representatives throughout the world

ISBN 978-0-230-49091-8

Original design by emc design limited
Page make-up by Mo Choy Design Ltd
All illustrations first published in *Academy Stars* Pupil's Book and Workbook unless otherwise stated.
Illustrations first published in *Happy Campers* Student's Book by Patricia Acosta and Angela Padrón: Drew Pocza (Make art) pp20, 28, 44, 52, 60, 68, 71, 73, 75, 77, 79, 81, 83, 85; Pronk Media Inc. pp12, 36, 71, 77
Illustrated by Tamara Joubert (in the style of Gareth Conway) (Beehive Illustration) pp8, 16, 24, 31, 32, 40, 48, 56, 64; Helen Prole (Plum Pudding Illustration Agency) pp4, 5, 9, 11, 13, 17, 18, 21, 23, 25, 29, 33, 35, 37, 41, 42, 43, 45, 47, 51, 53, 55, 57, 59, 61, 65, 66, 67, 69; David Shephard (in the style of Gareth Conway) (The Bright Agency) pp4(a), 6, 7, 14, 15, 22, 30, 31, 38, 46, 54, 62
Cover design by emc design limited
Cover photographs by **Getty Images**/Alberto Guglielmi (cm), Getty Images/Hero Images (bl)

The authors and publishers would like to thank the following for permission to reproduce their photographs:
Bananastock pp19(l, mr); Corbis p58(tr); **Getty Images**/iStockphoto Thinkstock Images/ Lalouetto p42(tl), Getty Images/Thinkstock Images/Hemera Technologies p26(tl); **ImageSource**/Charles Gullung p19(ml); **Macmillan Publishers Ltd**/Paul Bricknell pp19(r), 50(nose, ear, mouth, teeth, fingers); Macmillan Publishers Ltd/George Contorakes pp9(bl, br), 10(l, r), 12, 13(bl, br), 17(l, r), 18(l, r), 20, 26(cl, cr), 28, 29(l, r), 34(l, r), 36, 37(l, r), 41(l, r), 42(cl, cr), 44, 45(bl, br), 49, 50 (tl, tr, cl, cr, leg), 52, 53(bl, br), 57(l, r), 58(cl, cr), 60, 61(bl, br), 65(cl, cr), 66(cl, cr), 68, 69(bl, br); Macmillan Education Ltd/Haddon Davis p29(cr), 42(tr); Macmillan Education Ltd/Lisa Payne p29(cl); **Photodisc** pp26 (tr), 66(tl, tr); **Punchstock**/Rubberball p58(tl).

Printed and bound in Poland by CGS

2022 2021 2020 2019 2018

17 16 15 14 13 12 11 10 9 8